BASICS IN RHYTHM

An Instructional Text for All Intruments and Voice with Play-Along CD

by GARWOOD WHALEY

International Standard Book Number:
Book with 2 CDs: 978-1-57463-025-1
Book only: 978-1-57463-026-8
Printed and bound in U.S.A.

MEREDITH MUSIC PUBLICATIONS
a division of G.W. Music, Inc.
4899 Lerch Creek Ct., Galesville, MD 20765
http://www.meredithmusic.com

EXCLUSIVELY DISTRIBUTED BY

HAL•LEONARD®
CORPORATION
7777 W. BLUEMOUND RD. P.O. BOX 13819 MILWAUKEE, WI 53213

FOREWORD

Basics in Rhythm is a comprehensive collection of rhythm exercises for any instrument or voice in individual or group instruction. The purpose of this text is to introduce and develop the rhythms and rhythmic devices common to Western art and popular music from the Renaissance to the present.

Rhythm, the fundamental element of all music, is perhaps the most troublesome aspect of musical performance. This is especially true for beginning and intermediate instrumental and voice students since their concentration is divided between rhythm, pitch, expression, ensemble and technical skills. By isolating rhythm and employing a system of counting, this important musical element can be learned and mastered with out the interference of additional musical requirements.

This text provides a systematic approach to reading and understanding rhythm. Total mastery can be achieved through diligent practice and application of the materials presented within. It is my sincere hope that *Basics in Rhythm* will provide an enjoyable and educationally rewarding approach to the reading of rhythm.

G.W.

INTRODUCTION

Basics in Rhythm contains nine units of graduated rhythm exercises beginning with simple whole and half note studies and progressing through complex changing-meter exercises. The rhythm "key", which begins each study, presents important rhythmic material and should be mastered before proceeding to the following exercise.

PRACTICE METHOD
The rhythm exercises in this book are to be clapped and the syllables counted out loud. By counting out loud, the student will develop a system of "rhythm-syllable association". This system will enable the student to read rhythms at sight (regardless of the context or historical-style period). Repeat each measure of the rhythm "key" several times, or until mastered, before playing the rhythm exercise.

FUNDAMENTALS OF RHYTHM
Become familiar with the following fundamentals of rhythm. Mastery of the counting method through diligent practice will help the student to improve music reading skills.

NOTE VALUES AND RESTS

Notes	Names	Rests
o	Whole	▬
♩	Half	▬
♩	Quarter	𝄽
♪ (♫)	Eighth	𝄾
♬ (♬)	Sixteenth	𝄿
♬ (♬)	Thirty-second	𝅀

Notes	Names	Rests
o.	Dotted Whole	▬.
♩.	Dotted Half	▬·
♩.	Dotted Quarter	𝄽·
♪.	Dotted Eighth	𝄾·
♬.	Dotted Sixteenth	𝄿·
♬.	Dotted Thirty-second	𝅀·

- A *dot* after a note or rest adds half of the value of the note/rest it follows.

  Example: ♩. = ♩ + ♩   ♩. = ♩ + ♪

- A *second dot* after a note or rest adds half of the value of the first dot.

  Example: ♩.. = ♩ + ♩ + ♪   ♩.. = ♩ + ♪ + ♬

- A *tie* (curved line) connects two or more notes of the same pitch. Do not play (clap) the second note of a tie.

tie

TIME SIGNATURES
Most music is conveniently organized into *measures* (groups of beats) which are marked off by vertical *bar lines. Double bar lines* are used at the end of a large section of music or at the conclusion of a composition.

- A *time signature* consists of either two numbers arranged vertically or some other symbol. The *top number* tells how many counts or beats there are in each measure; any number may be used. The *bottom number* tells what kind of note value gets one count; only the following numbers may be used:

$$1\ o \quad 2\ ♩ \quad 4\ ♩ \quad 8\ ♪ \quad 16\ ♬ \quad 32\ ♬$$

- In *simple time* the beat unit is divisible by two. For example, $\frac{2}{4}$, $\frac{3}{4}$, $\frac{4}{4}$ and so on. The symbol for $\frac{4}{4}$ time or *common time* is **C**. The symbol for $\frac{2}{2}$ time or *cut time* is **¢**.

- In *compound time* the beat unit is divisible by three. For example, when $\frac{6}{8}$, $\frac{9}{8}$ and $\frac{12}{8}$ time signatures are used with fast tempos, the dotted quarter note gets one count. (When $\frac{6}{8}$, $\frac{9}{8}$ and $\frac{12}{8}$ time signatures are used with slow tempos, the eighth note gets one count.)

COUNTING METHOD

- When the quarter note receives one count ($\frac{2}{4}, \frac{3}{4}, \frac{4}{4}, \frac{5}{4}$, etc.), use the following measure-wise counting method (pronounced: one and two and three and four and):

- For the four-fold division of the beat (sixteenth notes) and its variations, use 1 e & a (pronounced: one ee and a):

- For the three-fold division of the beat and its variations, use 1 2 3, 4 5 6 ($\frac{6}{8}, \frac{9}{8}, \frac{12}{8}$ time when the dotted quarter note receives one count):

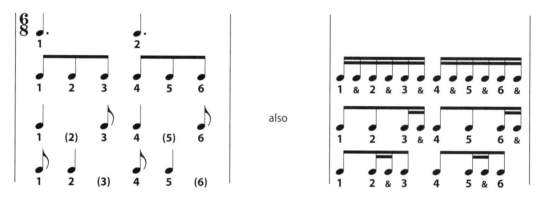

also

- The following examples illustrate how to count in time signatures that use the half note or eighth note as the beat unit:

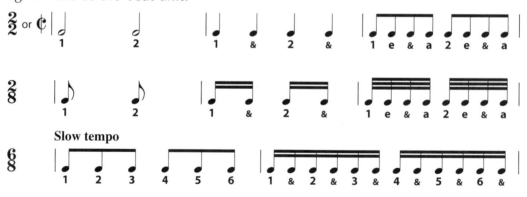

- A rhythm *triplet* occurs in music when three equal note values replace two equal note values:

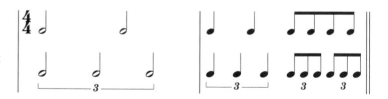

- In fast tempos, triplets can be counted but they must be kept equal.

(Do not confuse )

CONTENTS

UNIT 1

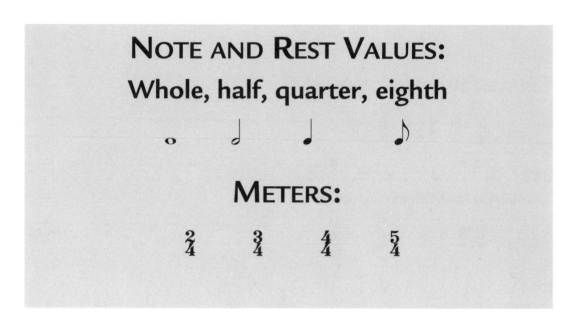

RHYTHM KEY 1

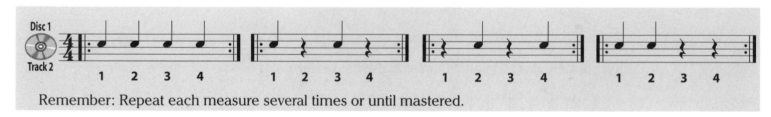

Remember: Repeat each measure several times or until mastered.

EXERCISE 1

RHYTHM KEY 2

EXERCISE 2

RHYTHM KEY 3

EXERCISE 3

RHYTHM KEY 4

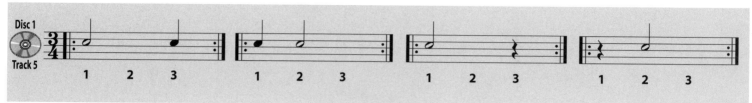

EXERCISE 4

RHYTHM KEY 5

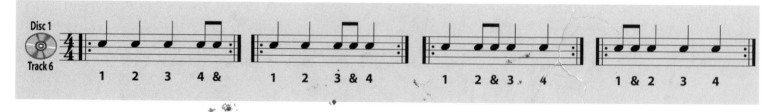

EXERCISE 5

RHYTHM KEY 6

EXERCISE 6

RHYTHM KEY 7

EXERCISE 7

RHYTHM KEY 8

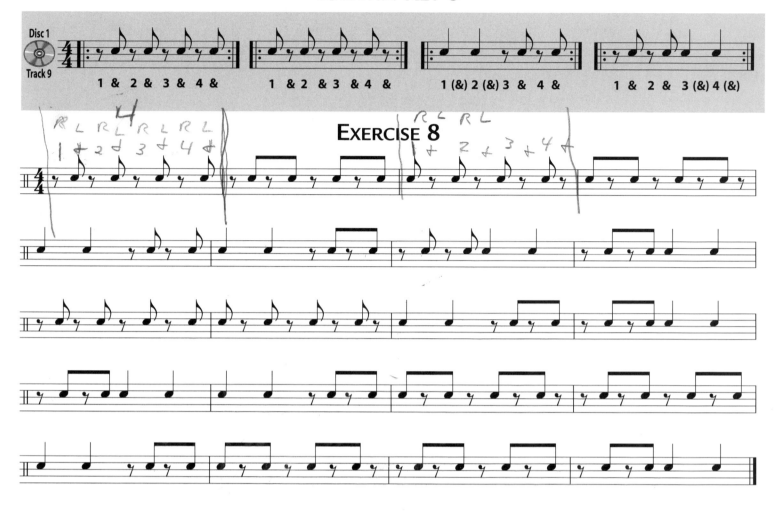

EXERCISE 8

RHYTHM KEY 9

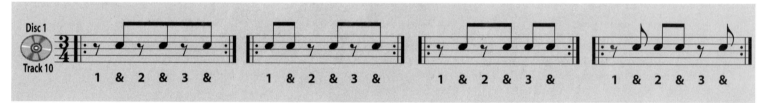

EXERCISE 9

RHYTHM KEY 10

EXERCISE 10

RHYTHM KEY 11

EXERCISE 11

UNIT 2

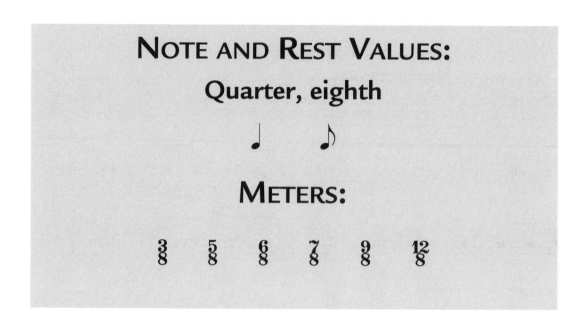

NOTE AND REST VALUES:
Quarter, eighth

METERS:

$\frac{3}{8}$ $\frac{5}{8}$ $\frac{6}{8}$ $\frac{7}{8}$ $\frac{9}{8}$ $\frac{12}{8}$

RHYTHM KEY 12

EXERCISE 12

RHYTHM KEY 13

EXERCISE 13

RHYTHM KEY 14

EXERCISE 14

RHYTHM KEY 15

EXERCISE 15

RHYTHM KEY 16

EXERCISE 16

RHYTHM KEY 17

EXERCISE 17

RHYTHM KEY 18

EXERCISE 18

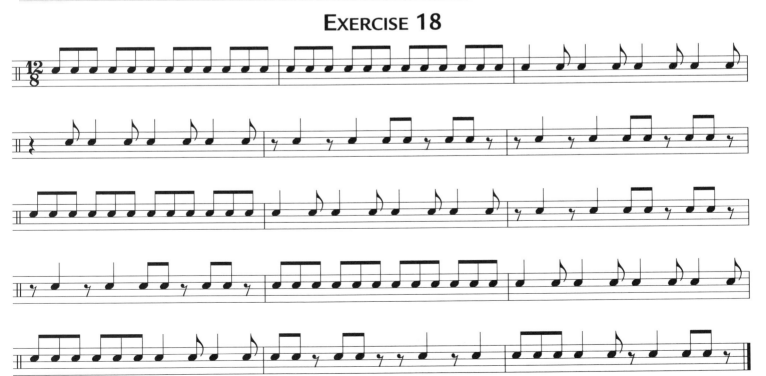

UNIT 3

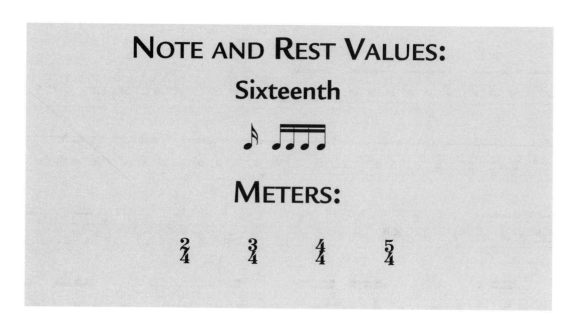

RHYTHM KEY 19

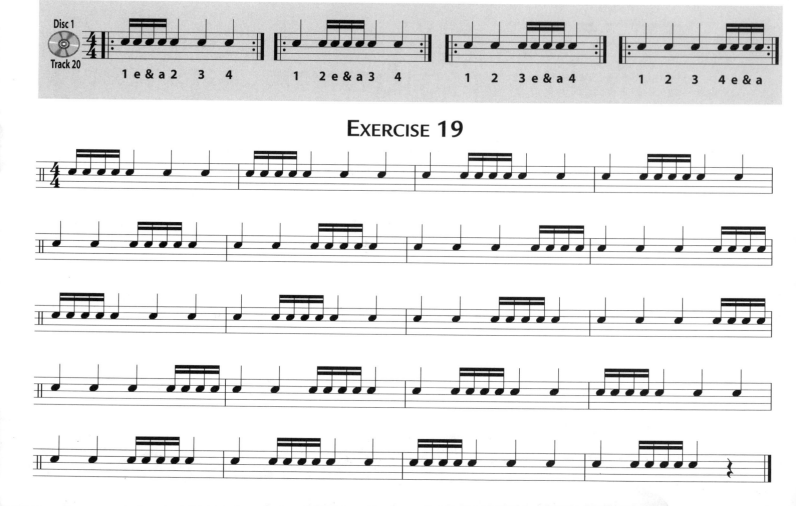

RHYTHM KEY 20

EXERCISE 20

RHYTHM KEY 21

EXERCISE 21

RHYTHM KEY 22

EXERCISE 22

RHYTHM KEY 23

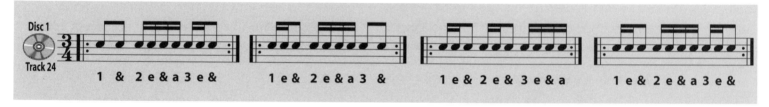

EXERCISE 23

RHYTHM KEY 24

EXERCISE 24

RHYTHM KEY 25

EXERCISE 25

RHYTHM KEY 26

EXERCISE 26

RHYTHM KEY 27

EXERCISE 27

RHYTHM KEY 28

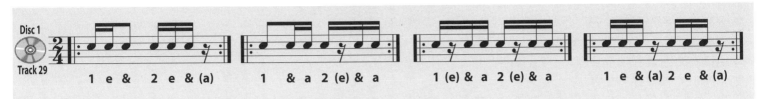

EXERCISE 28

RHYTHM KEY 29

EXERCISE 29

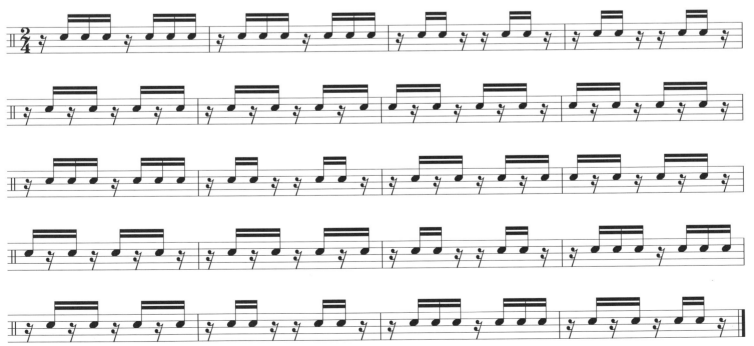

UNIT 4

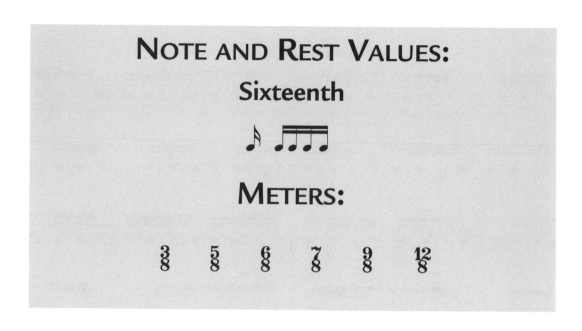

NOTE AND REST VALUES:

Sixteenth

METERS:

$\frac{3}{8}$ $\frac{5}{8}$ $\frac{6}{8}$ $\frac{7}{8}$ $\frac{9}{8}$ $\frac{12}{8}$

RHYTHM KEY 30

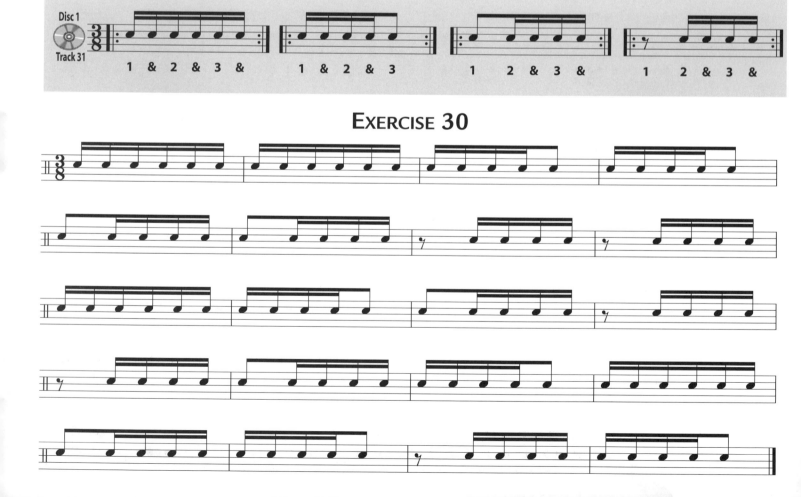

EXERCISE 30

RHYTHM KEY 31

EXERCISE 31

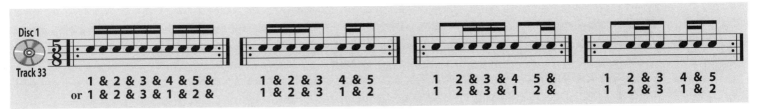

RHYTHM KEY 32

EXERCISE 32

RHYTHM KEY 33

EXERCISE 33

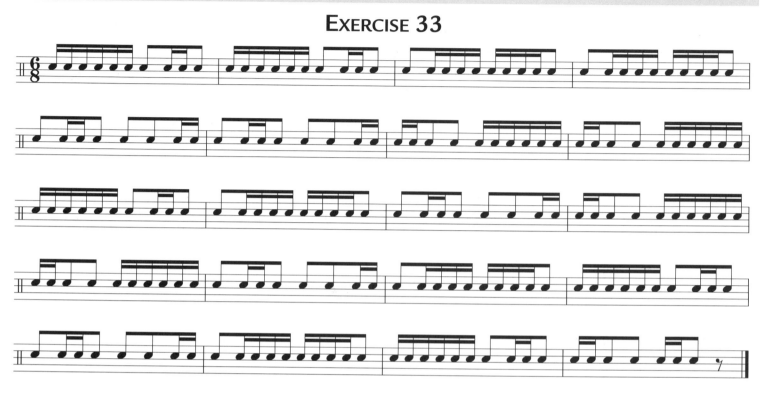

RHYTHM KEY 34

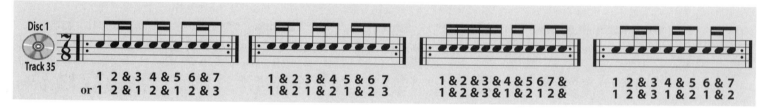

EXERCISE 34

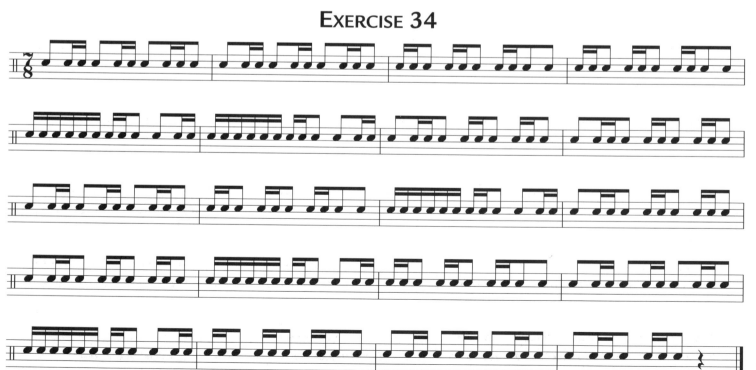

Rhythm Key 35

Exercise 35

Rhythm Key 36

Exercise 36

UNIT 5

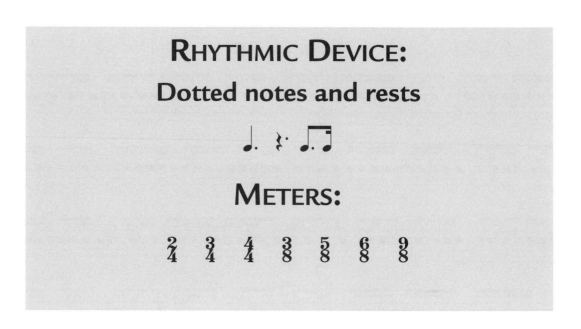

RHYTHM KEY 37

EXERCISE 37

RHYTHM KEY 38

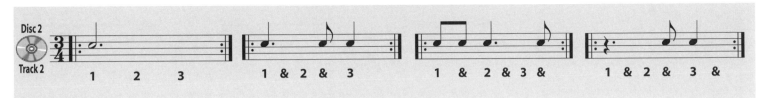

EXERCISE 38

RHYTHM KEY 39

EXERCISE 39

RHYTHM KEY 40

EXERCISE 40

RHYTHM KEY 41

EXERCISE 41

RHYTHM KEY 42

EXERCISE 42

RHYTHM KEY 43

EXERCISE 43

UNIT 6

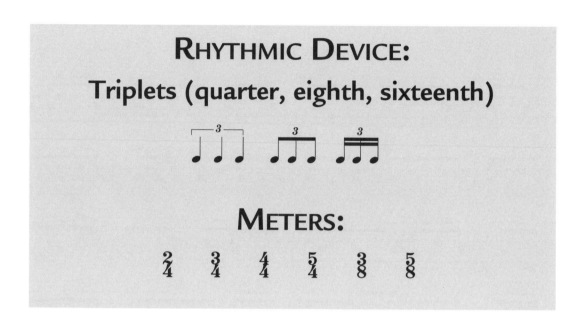

RHYTHM KEY 44

EXERCISE 44

Rhythm Key 45

Exercise 45

Rhythm Key 46

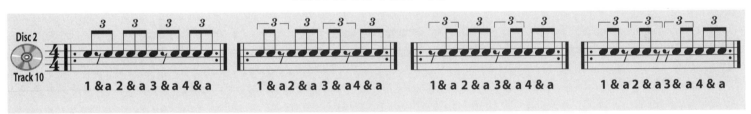

Exercise 46

RHYTHM KEY 47

EXERCISE 47

RHYTHM KEY 48

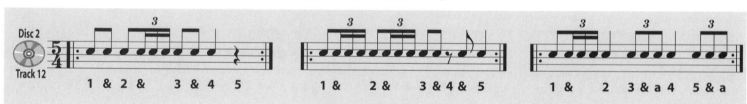

EXERCISE 48

RHYTHM KEY 49

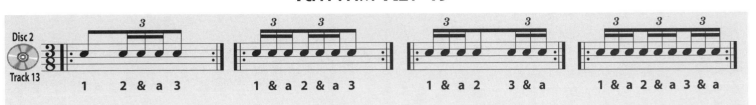

EXERCISE 49

RHYTHM KEY 50

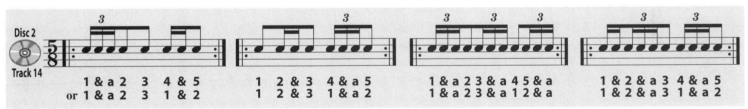

EXERCISE 50

UNIT 7

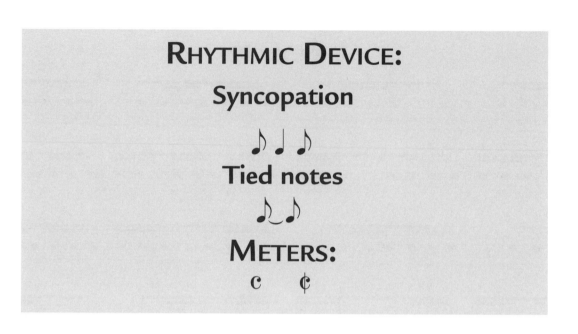

RHYTHM KEY 51

EXERCISE 51

RHYTHM KEY 52

EXERCISE 52

RHYTHM KEY 53

EXERCISE 53

RHYTHM KEY 54

EXERCISE 54

RHYTHM KEY 55

EXERCISE 55

RHYTHM KEY 56

EXERCISE 56

RHYTHM KEY 57

EXERCISE 57

UNIT 8

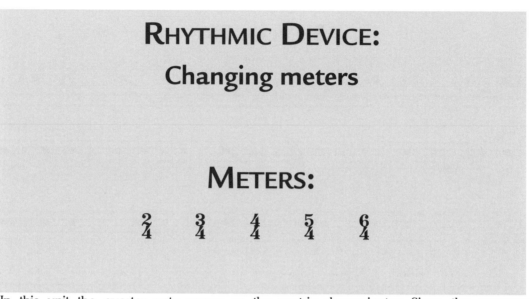

RHYTHMIC DEVICE:
Changing meters

METERS:

$\frac{2}{4}$ $\frac{3}{4}$ $\frac{4}{4}$ $\frac{5}{4}$ $\frac{6}{4}$

In this unit the quarter note serves as the metric denominator. Since the *common* denominator—quarter note—remains constant, it must be "felt" throughout each exercise.

RHYTHM KEY 58

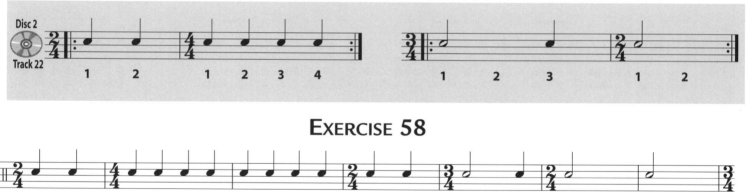

EXERCISE 58

RHYTHM KEY 59

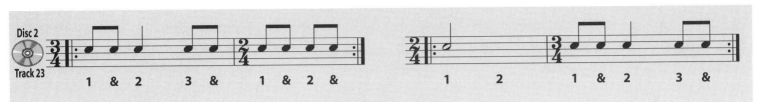

EXERCISE 59

RHYTHM KEY 60

EXERCISE 60

RHYTHM KEY 61

EXERCISE 61

RHYTHM KEY 62

EXERCISE 62

RHYTHM KEY 63

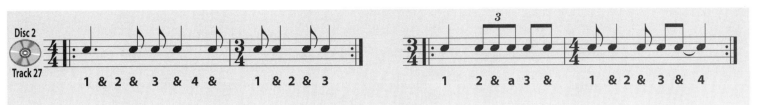

EXERCISE 63

RHYTHM KEY 64

EXERCISE 64

UNIT 9

RHYTHMIC DEVICE:
Changing meters

METERS:

$$\frac{2}{4} \quad \frac{3}{4} \quad \frac{4}{4} \quad \frac{2}{8} \quad \frac{3}{8} \quad \frac{5}{8} \quad \frac{6}{8} \quad \frac{7}{8} \quad \frac{2}{16} \quad \frac{3}{16} \quad \frac{4}{16} \quad \frac{5}{16}$$

In this unit the eighth note serves as the metric denominator. Since the *common* denominator—eighth note—remains constant, it must be "felt" throughout each exercise. (On page 47 of this unit the sixteenth note serves as the metric denominator and must be "felt" throughout each study.)

RHYTHM KEY 65

EXERCISE 65

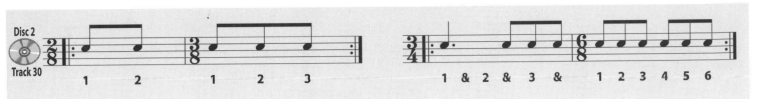

RHYTHM KEY 66

EXERCISE 66

RHYTHM KEY 67

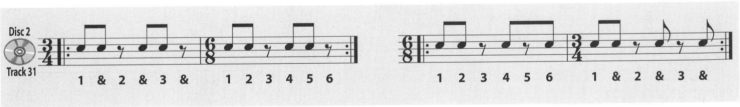

EXERCISE 67

44

RHYTHM KEY 68

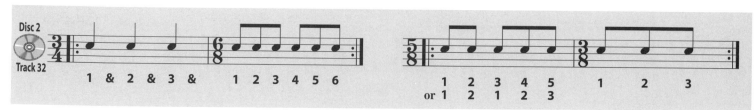

EXERCISE 68

RHYTHM KEY 69

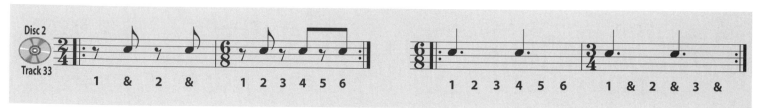

EXERCISE 69

RHYTHM KEY 70

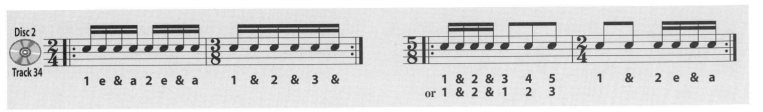

EXERCISE 70

RHYTHM KEY 71

EXERCISE 71

RHYTHM KEY 72

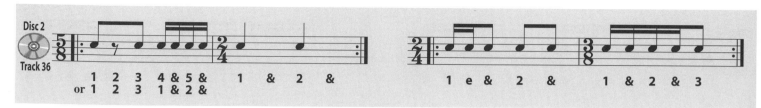

EXERCISE 72

RHYTHM KEY 73

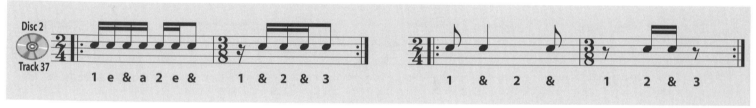

EXERCISE 73

Rhythm Key 74

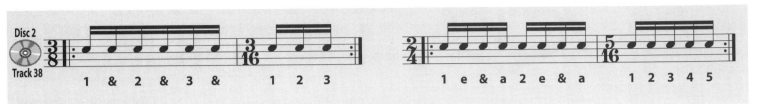

Exercise 74

Rhythm Key 75

Exercise 75

MORE GREAT BOOKS FROM MEREDITH MUSIC

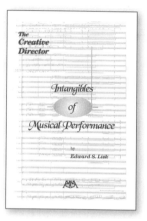

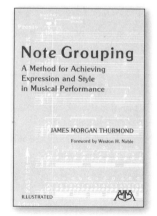